POETRY

A VERSE PLAY

FICTION

D1525932

STORY LINE PRESS

For Michael Glaser 4/88

Family Life

poems by Colette Inez

In poetry —

Colette Inez

Story Line Press

1988

THIS SERIES IS
MADE POSSIBLE BY THE GENEROUS SUPPORT
of the
NICHOLAS ROERICH MUSEUM, NEW YORK

•

ISBN: 0-934257-12-4

•

Published by Story Line Press
A subsidiary of The Reaper, Inc.
325 Ocean View Avenue
Santa Cruz, California 95062

•

Book Design by Lysa Howard-McDowell
Typesetting by The Type Factory

Acknowledgements

My thanks to the John Simon Guggenheim Memorial Foundation for its generous support. And to the corporation of Yaddo, The Virginia Colony of the Creative Arts, Ragdale Foundation and the Leighton Art Colony, Banff Center, School of Fine Arts for residencies which allowed me to complete this book.

Special thanks to Charlotte Mandel for her encouragement and critical comments on the manuscript.

The poems in this book originally appeared, some in slightly different form, in these publications whose editors I would like to thank.

Virginia Quarterly Review "Gascon Journey," "Red August Letter," "Animal Nature" *(Monitor Book Anthology & Yearbook of American Poetry,* 1983)
The Reaper "Meeting in Nérac"
Cincinnati Review "Papal Saw in a Roman Bind," "Skymyths"
Mid-America Review "Tunnel Songs"
Devil's Millhopper "Event Horizons"
Crosscurrents "Orphans of Tangshan"
Confrontation "Lost Daughters at School"
West Branch "Without Toys at the Home," "Musing on Large Questions in a Small Corner of England"
Poetry Northwest "Escape from the Iron Gates," "What Are the Days" (Pushcart Prize, 1986)
Cafeteria "My Father Sails in the West"
Graham House Review "Sock Poem"
Boulevard "Setting Out from the Lowlands"
Memphis Review "The Dreamforest"
Salmagundi "Seasons of the War"
Three Rivers Review "Windpipe and Life Go On Song"
Beyond Baroque "Dee is Conjured Up and Sent Away"
Hunter Magazine "Ray"
Minnesota Review "Family Life"
Massachusetts Review "Hearing New Year's Eve"
Caliban "The Happy Child," "Going Far"
Harvard Review "Reading Tu Fu, I Wait for My Husband"
Helicon Nine "Probings under Vega"
Panoply "Winter Modes"
Mudfish "After the Cantata Sounds Its Last Alleluia," "The Day We Made Long Shadows"

Books by Colette Inez

The Woman Who Loved Worms (1972)
Alive and Taking Names (1977)
Eight Minutes from the Sun (1983)
Family Life (1988)

Even more for Saul again

Rue Chant D'Oiseau, Brussels, Belgium

Bayview Avenue, Merrick, Long Island

Off Central Park West, New York City

Rue Chant D'Oiseau, Brussels, Belgium

GASCON JOURNEY

I have set out to meet her
for the last time, to examine
a face that resembles mine
in one corner above the right eye
and in a temple vein.
Fontainebleu, Tours, Poitiers,
Angoulême. The train feeds
the voyager a dream of calm.
My mother and father, their secrets
hummed like rails, flew through
road beds and coupling cars.
Unlikely lovers.
"I'd almost forgotten," she will sigh.
"Why do you persist?" She won't look
into my eyes. I'll watch her turn away
after I leave. A flutter of a memory
too swift to catch will vanish in a meadow,
a corridor of trees. Was it her face
bent over my crib? Were her shoulders
hunched when she whispered to the priest?
What did she confess to him?
I almost see her, my rare and somber visitor,
the mother nuns said was a cousin or an aunt.
The long aisle of lies. I also sigh. I,
unknown to the few of a thinning clan,
have come this far to see a blood stranger.
Bordeaux, Agen, Nérac, Espiens.
There are questions I will never ask.
There are answers she will never give.

MEETING IN NÉRAC

My mother's face, a lantern at the window
lights a path to her door, to openings I hear
in her voice asking me to climb the stairs
to her booklined rooms.

I try to read the small print of her lips.
She turns away like a page too quickly skimmed.
The parchment of her skin whispers a story
of two scholars humbled by illicit love,
my lettered sires who signed me away.

When she crosses slowly to the room's far end
and perches on a brown wing chair, she is a queen
in ravelled sleeves who offers me a Baedeker
and the history of her town.
What she won't say floods the room with images:

she is naked, heavy breasts graze the water
as she wades into the river. In a shadowy cove,
the body swims languorously, one arm, then another
pulling her forward to the far shore.
There my father writes marginal notes on the edges
of a manuscript. He will comb her wet hair.
She will hum a song.

"How long is your holiday?" I am pulled short
from my musings by her voice. "The region is filled
with interesting ruins." Her English accent rings
in counterpoint with the sigh of palms on her red
tiled roof, in the south of France

where we speak after a long absence of years.
"Next year Halley's Comet returns" I say.
She recalls its glow and how she tugged at her father's
arm alongside the same blue-shuttered house
in which we talk of traveling
through the mother country.

Ruler of wanderers and lanterns at night, let her study
the comet one more time. I ask this for a woman of Nérac
from whom I inherit a love of quandaries: my doubt
of heaven, hers of the here and now. What else we meant
to call into question or deny stays unresolved
like an unfocused star.

THE PAPAL SAW IN A ROMAN BLIND

I can almost hear the bells
rung by the priest who sired a child.
Nuncio, let that father rise
to sit at my right touch. One last
kiss to ease his grief in the afterlife.

I, his bastard, bid for calm
like a Papal See in a murmur of signs.
Confessor, hear my doubts of the Seven
Dolors of Mary, Elevation of the Host.
I can see the church walking

on its knees and offer my alms
to a ghost who cannot see the weight
of years, blood-soaked stones and
the orphanage drilling its wards
on the telling of beads.

My father, does he hear the lambs
bleating the hundredth psalm
of man's praise to God? Vicar of Christ,
here is a silver monstrance, here is
a chasuble of gold to pay for his release.

All our wrongs take refuge in the hospice
of time. I make this offering to lift up
my father's heart out of his remains,
mysterious as particles of light
flooding the earth from the sun.

TUNNEL SONGS

Engraved by rain
my father's stone
marks a body
turning in a world
he used as he could.

I was not made lightly
when he and my mother wept
dark tunnels in an iron bed.

Rain on his grave
writes nothing
in a language I can read.

When I was born my mother
hid me in a paragraph.
"No one will notice
if she doesn't cry," she said
running to confess
failure in orthography.

Now she lives like a stone
in her sister's garden.
The rain prepares a speech
to write on her face
in the winter.

When she sleeps I will feel
her turning
in my bed of parentheses
in my house of lost rhymes.

EVENT HORIZONS

1

A flame crests in the fireplace.
Loose ashes and flurries of snow scatter
in a California winter.
The caped figure, hurried up the stairs,
is the midwife who eases my father
into dawn. Heavy velvet drapes are drawn.
Grandfather twirls a brandy glass and
lifts it to the light. A son to carry
his likeness and his name, their names
emblazoned in gold letters on a door.
He draws on a cigar, watches a cloud
of smoke rise and disperse. A tiny bubble sits
on the baby's lips, then breaks. Sleep.
Soon to receive his first dream, the boy
is ignorant of boundaries and time. He
has not learned the meaning of a quarter
of an hour, fenced-in lives, exceptions
and rules, encircled troops. He is one
with his desires. The horizon line of that moment
will never cross the light again, not its
intersections nor frontiers, not in the earth
where his body will transform into mole blood
and roots.

2

Almond trees are espaliered on either side
of the twisting road. Behind boxed hedges,
the garden withdraws into a trace of fragrances.
But once inside the house, these languors stop.
The maid dusts, mops, sweeps, plumps up pillows
whose slips are tatted with ivory lace.
Cousins assist in the delivery
with cool, damp cloths, a whiff of camphor and lilac
cologne. Birth is women's work, they say.
My mother in summer needs no coaxing to arrive
in the afternoon's aroma of lavender and mint,
fresh linen sheets. She takes the soft, white
contours as her due, a natural state
in the center of her wants. On the verandah,
the household's former only child
spills lemon tea on her pinafore.
"Where is papa?" she sobs and wipes her nose
with the back of her hand. Under a blue glaze of sky
the men are away in the towns buying and selling
olives and wine. Their ancestors, gazing out
of oval frames, seem to bask in a glow of calm days.
Slow hours. Peeping through a frill,
my grandmother's nipple trickles milk the baby sips,
transfixed. This episode's horizon line wavers
and a powdered ash of roses sifts and blows into snow.

3

Snow melts on a clock's face whose hands
advance with the light of stars. In a climate
spared extremes, snow is a rare visitor and
leaves nothing but a tracery of loosely
remembered days in fading frames. Does my
mother remember the buttons she undid,
one by one, when she counted contractions and
her time had come? Does she recall the sky, white
as the chart and certificate that recorded
my birth? When I was born my mother prayed
I would be pardoned for giving testimony
to her intense desire. Mary, Mother of God,
was her mother then, blessed among women,
the one she called to when I pushed my way
out of her womb into an unwed mother's ward.

Snow, the boundary point of some far off
event dissolving when the owl roosted
in the cedar, its castings of mousehair
and bones, gray pellets of dust on the ground,
snow dimming the light in chapel when I knew
the feel of smudged rosaries, four taps
on my body, the sign of the cross, professing
faith in Our Father, God, Mary, Mother of God,
Son and a Holy Ghost I could not find
in corridors where I stepped in unison, a child
in uniform engaged in small wars lost against
touching myself, wrong intent, glib speech.
Slowly, I learned to say what I thought
all wanted to hear: *mea culpa*, I regret
not being pure under a snow of bloomers and bibs,
cowls and flannel gowns flapping on a line
drawn against clouds whose edges blur and drift
in a fog of childhood rituals.

4

Belgium offers up its miles of plateaus,
polders, rivers, exhausted veins of coal in
the Borinage, and in the Ardennes, limestone
cliffs and wooded hills. On the outskirts
of Brussels, in the province of Brabant,
shrubs squat in a land whose horizon line
refused to disappear. My parents have vanished
to live elsewhere at opposite ends of continents.
I ask the nuns for them but no one says they
will never arrive nor why they should shift
their lives around. When my father dies, I am not
told. Did Mother Superior know? One day
holds another in its nest. Spring. Summer. Fall.

Dry snow falls on a skating rink where the wards
have come to scrawl their clumsy penmanship on ice.
I glide beyond the calls to form a line and leave.
Shifting limits, turns and frames. In a province
of lost origins where borders fold one into another
and trail off, the child I tap on the shoulder
turns to me with my own face and we know
we will escape the custody of the past,
giving astonishment a horizon line not yet
defined but waiting to be drawn.

THE ORPHANS OF TANGSHAN

After the earthquake of 1976 numerous surviving children found in the rubble were too young to know their family names.

The thunder has no mother.
Who is the father of the wind?
In the sky the Mother of the Seven Stars
gives honey to The Bear.
The orphanage children begin to speak.

A boy mutters earth has swallowed
his name and points at the ground.
Ghost sister, a girl shouts in her sleep.
The land ate my house, she says when she wakes.

After the earthquake, they are given new names.
Who are your parents? visitors ask
and, do you love the party and the state?
Our teachers, they reply and yes, yes.

Calendars are hung and curled into scrolls,
quilts open and fold. Each day bowls
fill up with rice, white as the paper
that holds brushed words.

Years crumble and fall down, the children
get up and grow tall yet many keep stumbling
inside the same dream: a red sun spills them
into dawn when the city of Tangshan
eases out of sleep and across the northern valley
mothers call Moon Willow, Monkey,
time to wake.

LOST DAUGHTERS AT SCHOOL

Once there was the reek of inkwells
in a Gascony school where my mother
was indentured to scrawling "la plume"
and "le crayon" over and over in the pages
of a lined, softback blue book, her fastidious
ear catching the scratch of the pen's nib
as it ascended into blue, angular loops,
and the blurred melody of pencils even at
a sharpened point humming gray cadences.
Such were the songs of implements
in her first days.

What she went on to write at her oakwood
desk is mostly lost in a crumple of blotted
lesson plans designed to teach the mother
tongue. Her name at the top of the page
began each enterprise of ciphers
and orthography.

I see her in the school's cramped rooms
at four o'clock shaking a film of chalk
out of her blue marino skirt.
She is the slow and cautious one,
hunched, clutching a bookbag, the last to cross
the bridge with the stragglers into town.
Drowsy eyes, thin, half-parted lips, her face holds
its look of astonishment for moments
at a time. A girl from the south accustomed
to grapes and apricots, she grows, goes north
and studies the art of manuscripts.

When I was sent to school, I, too, knuckled
under a fist of words although they belonged
to another mother tongue. "Plume" in my
second language meant a cluster of feathers,
and crayons had waxy points that slept
in a yellow box.

When I think of my mother as a girl,
it is from a long arc across the ocean
into a shimmer of days just after the century's turn,
before she fell under the shadow of the church
and the red-haired priest from America.

Upon arriving in America
I still remember writing my name on a slate,
the white unsteady forms of the curves
and strokes, COLETTE, not after Sidonie Gabrielle
but in honor of the founder of Poor Clares,
Saint Colette, chaste and rigorous in her
habits of obedience.

WITHOUT TOYS AT THE HOME

No dolls, nuns thought we would
quarrel, no spinning tops, tin
what-have-yous, wind-ups, anything
which might distract offsprings
of the solemn church. Nuns meant
well as did their priests mumbling
over games of chess.

At the Home, I gave my fingernails names
and jobs: old thumb, Pierre, the cop,
pinkie Francine, slim-hipped, one-note
pianist.

In my palms I loved the roads
that led me to my realms: Lantasah, high
in the reaches of Ti, Whoa and Neigh,
crofts for my shires, stallions and nags.

The rockinghorse I wanted lived in a yellow
book where a boy arranged trains
on the floor. His sister held a china doll
with lambswool yellow hair. I let my playstone
sleep in the doll's chiffonier, in a velvet-
lined drawer.

At the Home, our beds used to float like yachts
in the waves of our sleep. My sheet was a sail,
the pillow, a horse I rode calling to my second
finger, Dulce: "Stay away, nuns will find us
in my cloud."

A cloud won't stay put. More than once I've
been found out. My cheeks still smart from
being caught. Spring clouds, war clouds,
summer thunder, lulls and calms. Behind the gate
of the Home, the children have fallen in a mumble
of years, and their children have toys enough to
break, and their children enough for quarreling.

ESCAPE FROM THE IRON GATES

When we squatted by a puddle and wrote our names
on water with a stick, you curved "n" twice. Anne.
I crossed my "t's" as they rose.
The reflected sky trembled with our signatures.

Our angels were white clouds on the pond.
Their shadows trailed us and the winged caps of nuns.
How would we ride through the iron gates?
You wished for a donkey like the beast our Lord rode
in Jerusalem. Rather a white charger, I thought,
fit for a lady.

At night I rode my white pillow, moved my thighs
against its flanks in that damp, half-sleep the children
pulled over themselves like a coverlet.

Scrubbed nuns' faces in white cowls. Like moons they gleamed
at the end of long lines we formed to pray and study God.
No mirrors allowed. Anne, you searched for your face in the tops
of shoes. I greeted mine at the bottom of a bowl. Clutching our
rosaries, we kissed The Virgin's stony lips. Did she read my
carnal thoughts?

Angels still trumpet over Belgian fields. Years dart like birds
in and out of gates we have learned to open and to lock.
Surely, three-way, hand, full-length mirrors have not cracked
nor clouded over in rooms with our pillows and books, writings
and monograms on linen.

Somewhere, you arrange your blond hair into a cloud.
I shall never see your face again when I look into the water.
Your name's one syllable vanished with each letter's stroke.
Anne, shadowy-pale.

White pillow, our childhood on a ship, snowdeep by the pond.
My impure longings. The old disgrace brushes my face awake.

MY FATHER SAILS IN THE WEST, DWELLING PLACE OF DEPARTED SOULS

Ghost-priest now moored to a solar bark
chanting spells to get back your name,
the memory of a gliding life,
before you were called by the Judge of the Dead,
did you sing here on the water,
in the fulfilling long light
that comes before dusk?

My seminarian, the abbots praised your summer
conduct at St. Mary's-on-the-Sea, what zest you brought
to loving God. Did you sing "The Seven Joys
of Mary," or the "Devil's Nine Questions"
when you pulled on the oars?

Sailor, where the dead ride at anchor and have no shore,
my father, these many years later I carry your face
to reflect on the water. Do you hear my song?
It will follow your wake. Save me a place
at the prow of the bark.

ANIMAL NATURE

When my mother mulls on the nature
of angels, ether and clouds, I put
down my fork and study a fly,
its wingtips on my mutton chop,
before me a stack of plates to be
wiped clean like words on a slate.
Even in silence as I do the work
I lose an argument with her, I, her
bastard daughter.

Slice off her head, tie up her tongue.
Tell her she's another captive
to the brooding of daughters eating
their mothers' grievances.

"We'll all arrive in a world of light
beyond desire," she goes on to explain
how faith gives way to perfect love
in the afterlife.

Sometimes, when I see her
in the mirror, full-breasted and
intense, I start to believe
I was made from her animal nature.

My mother in the looking glass,
behind her the dark like an idle rumor
of nothingness devouring our lives.

SOCK POEM

Fill my sock with motherwit and thrift.
Crybaby. Ninny. Yes, I was. My papa had a lady
love. Uhuh. Where's your papa now?
He's in a box of prayerbooks.

What's your mama doing now? She's darning up
the past. Soon she'll think its perfect: none
of the patches show. "What was his name?"

She turns to her sister who remembers the garden
in Gascony, their rattled mother and her adages:
Take heed of men with close-set eyes.
They will melt in a winter of homilies.

A penny moon is nothing saved, is a coin of a light.
My little birth was time well spent in a bank
of events. Bank on the future costing more
than facts, the aforesaid rules of forgetfulness.

My papa loved or mama did not. Men, their smell
of chemicals. A raveled past on the outskirts of town
weaving in the syllables. They cleared their throats
and I was made alive to fill an empty year.

"You all come back real soon," the Mother Superior
said in my reverie, and I ran and I ran with a penny's worth
of mothering, and my papa's face round as the moon.

SETTING OUT FROM THE LOWLANDS

Do buildings in America grow taller
than Saint Julian's?
What will eat you when you drown?
The questions swirled
as the gate unlocked,
and hungry to be noticed
in my new, red dress,
embroidered flowers at the gathered neck,
I left them in the afternoon,
a child singled out for departure
at the start of the war,
before tanks
bulldozed the Do Not Trespass signs
in the capital.

Nuns in black and white,
children in weekday brown
waved me goodbye. Birdsong Street,
Brussels, Belgium, farewell.
"Come see us when you're a fine lady,"
a child blew a kiss
that flew over paths
straight as the rule of nuns
who kept us in line for the Liturgy
of the Eucharist, Midday Prayer,
the daily chanting at Evensong.

Who would eat my morning gruel,
sing my praise to God at Lauds?
What kept the ship afloat?
A great fish? I expected no less
than such miracles.

In America I have made the sign
of the cross in buildings
taller than Saint Julian's
and sailed into years
beyond that child's imagining
of a fine lady come back to gloat
in the Children's Home
whose corridors caught echoes
from small, red mouths
that set whispers afloat,
calling "pray for us, pray for us."

Bayview Avenue, Merrick, Long Island

THE DREAMFOREST

The photo shows a backdrop of roaring falls and a plain child
who stands wary of the railing against which she leans.
Will it give way to an abyss billowing up plumes
of white horsetails? Will she stroke the fur of creatures
in a dreamforest where she loses who she is, a child
among people not wanting her reflection in their mirror?

"She stands there and gawks at their door," thin grandmother
nibbles melba toast. "Too late to send her back with the war
going on," fat grandmother pours cream on her shredded wheat.

"Did you see those pictures?" Thin grandmother notes
the harried faces of her son and his wife who'd gone all day
without a drink. "And this one of the child in front
of the falls? Look how she scowls."

"They had no business taking her," fat grandmother thinks
of the silver cocktail shaker reflecting her daughter's
manicure, her perfect clothes. "The child's a mistake,"
the women nod in rare accord.

In the same room, the child gobbles waxy American toast.
She's learned a language of turned backs, locked doors,
but not the trick of English words
which loop from mouth to mouth like moths,
maps on their wings she can't yet read
in the same way she is baffled by small print
on a matchbox, or the wrapper on a loaf of Silvercup.

She decides she will speak to the Moon of the Shambling Bear.
In her dreamforest. He will command: Mirror, show four
trapped bodies in the flames, toast-colored horses to pull
the hearse to and from the funeral. And show our girl
full-length, beautiful and cold, so rich in words,
she will fling them one by one into the roaring falls.

SEASONS OF THE WAR

For foster mother, Ruth

In the foggy spring of the far off war,
what could I have given her?
A wind-up doll instead of the child
the doctor told her might cure pinched
nerves, migraines, a fraying marriage
of fifteen years. What did she want?

I wanted her amber pomade, lip balm,
lotions, and lilac cologne, little jars
of rouge, vanishing creams, the lie
of "you are beautiful."

In the summer of the war,
on our porch with the blue glider
and white wicker chairs, what did she want?
Another start? Another drink? A body
not tricking her with blissful dreams
of mothering?

I longed to step into her paisley dress
with the fringed epaulets, to button
her yellow silk blouse, black birds on it.
I wanted them to fly out of her small breasts,
to sing to us in the morning.

In the stormy fall of the year,
I found her naked body in the hall.
"One too many," someone said. I'd seen the shot
glasses lined up on the bar downstairs
where she sat on a stool that spun
like a record on a phonograph.

Rhumba tunes pulsed softly
when she convalesced. In her peach robe
and matching bandeau pulling back her hair,
how fragile she was and inconsolable.

I envied her cream of tomato soup,
orange pekoe tea, the red laquered tray
with parasols stenciled in gold.
They were close to her.

"What can I do?" I wanted to run to the store for her.
"Go comb your hair," I was dismissed.
She'd return to exposés in True Confessions,
Silver Screen.

I stole her tortoise shell mirror,
her apple green comb
in the winter when F.D.R. declared war here.
She huddled by the radio,
sipping double scotches, straight.
"My nerves are raw," she'd sigh
and drape a hand across her eyes.
I learned to tiptoe up the stairs.

The war streaked headlines, dark bands
of birds, flying in a line.
Spring came. Summer. One day
she didn't answer to her name.

I thought I could have caught her last breath
in the tortoise shell mirror,
parted her hair with the apple green comb.

She was laid out in a beige
lace gown, lavender sash, her face,
a peaceful mask but I stood by the casket
in a pink, puffed dress and choked back rage
as if it were a bone stuck in my throat.

Later, alone in her room, I did a rhumba
with her empty clothes, held on to the sleeves,
imagined her soul lolling on the deck
of a Caribbean party boat.
And I combed and combed my hair.

I RECALL "D" MY FOSTER FATHER'S
SECOND WIFE AND HER NOTES TO ME

Dollé, the name your baby nurse gave you
thinking it meant doll in French, still flashes
in my memory, and I see your penmanship again,

straight up and down, an angry wire, above the stem
of your slashed "i's", the looped dots, a vanity
repeated in your jewel-studded wedgies,
gold-tipped cigarettes.

Spring memory. On my bed you have left a note
in a pale pink envelope on which you do not
write my name. "See me at once." The "D" at the end
of your folded script is like a bullet
from an arsenal where your messages are stored.
My throat is tight. I tap at your door.

You stride towards me in a beige,
big-shouldered dress, metallic chips
ranked in rows along the neck, and down the arms.
Clenching a rum and coke in a chilled, tall glass,

you say you want to kill me for sneaking off with a boy
to the beach. I try to explain. "How dare you talk back,
get out," you spit, kick my shin, crack my tooth
with your shoe. Blood in my mouth, I back away

from you, step by step, down the stairs.
"Your own mother didn't want you."
You save that for last.
I am pushed out the door into cold rain,
and sleep in a neighbor's garage.

Autumn memory. I come in the house,
hungry from raking leaves. On the kitchen table
in a stiff, white sealed envelope, your note
explodes: "I have padlocked the refrigerator door.
This is the last time you will ever take my food."

Dollé, Mrs. B., even now I remember
how you capped your capital "M's"
with a black horizontal line, three bars beneath it
like a prison window,
your "B", two jagged peaks tipped
on their sides, and what you wrote me
in still another season,
each crackling curve of word:

"I have reason to believe you have used my perfume.
You are a liar and a thief."

WINDPIPE AND LIFE GO ON SONG

Foster mother Dee
gripped my windpipe
with her thumbs.
Fear dried out my mouth.
Grandma called: police.

Dee stopped
to down another shot of rum.
I touched a blue path around my neck
and spun into fog.

That night the police
knocked on the door of my dream.
When I sawed off Dee's head,
they hooked their thumbs
into Sam Brown belts.

In the blue days of getting back
my voice,
what did Grandma say while I moped
with my head in my hands?
"Don't sit there like a leech."

And life went on and on
like a long-winded speech.
Dee fattened and drooped,
broke off, made up with Ray,
Grandma's son.

I saw Ray's thing
like a billy club
sticking out of his pants.
He'd give me a spit-filled kiss
I'd wipe away with the back of my hand.

In the gray days of choking
the fire to dig out my books
burned in a drunken binge,

the great Homer tapped on the door
of my dream. "Go build a raft
for the lattermost isles"
he counseled me

before Ray took off
and grandma had a fall
and I bought a blue dress
for her burial.

In the green days of leaving
Dee to toss off
whiskies in a sour house,
I embarked

for another town
to look for a well-stocked bar
on a banker's yacht I didn't find
and life went on and on.
It went on.

DEE IS CONJURED UP AND SENT AWAY

It was a time for the queen to break
crockery in our dinky kitchen.
Out spun a plate, a cup, a bowl.
"I want each and every piece picked up.
Do you hear?" Her eyes bulged like a frog's.
A tadpole, I swam in a pool of broken glass,
humming who knows what. I lived in a swamp
of cadences out of tune with her domain.

Plumed smoke curled from her mouth.
She was my volcano. I wished her hellfire
in a dream where she was supposed to plummet
into flames, but she couldn't shake off
her mother's cold, her father's downpour
of stones, and lived on.

What is there to say in the face of these tears
whose memory I carry in a jar? I could never
make her tell the glassblower's secret
for destroying his work, and failed to lull
her rampages, to shrug off days
when she wouldn't speak. It is time to close the book
on the queen.

The last time I looked she was a hill, raggedy and loose.
And the last time I looked, she was a jar
holding the ashes of our quarrels, and the last time
I looked she was dust.

ABSOLVING YOU

For Nana

I and my zero face
quivered in the mirror and sighed.
We were not about to dematerialize
although you'd said: "You're nothing
and won't amount to much."

How could nothing be much?
I learned to mull on paradox
and tried to tote up what my body
might fetch, the penny's worth
of chemicals.

"You'd better learn to sew,"
you stared past me when you spoke.
I stitched up your mouth
in my fantasy of bliss.

And later on, in a home-made dress,
I stood beside your corpse,
pulled the rings from your fingers;
for once, you kept a civil tongue,
my icy-eyed appraiser,
tough to the dingy, fly-specked end
in the charity ward of the hospital,

you, who are almost nothing now,
the puncture mark of a lost stitch
I trace in a dream
of altering a crooked seam,
of mending the past.

RAY

Ray, the seller of silks from Chicago,
did the mambo, the foxtrot, the rhumba,
the samba, the conga.
Narrow feet in silk-blend socks, two-toned
shoes. Slim, in flannel slacks, tapered shirts,
all of him sashayed and twirled.
He didn't miss a step. A smooth man.
Confident

except when his hands danced the hangover shake,
and he blinked back dreams
of tapping spiders with jittery legs
dangling from a web.

Ray, the seller of silks.
A bolt of crepe de chine, madame, he said
as he winked with a sweep of his hand
to conjure up grand distances
where women lounged on ottomans
and a man had only to point.
Ray from Chicago.

And he loved a well-turned ankle, seamed hose,
women who floated on clouds of perfume.
After closing the sale, he smoothed his hair
in the mirror and hummed,
except when his mouth burned for a shot
of rye, bourbon, neat, whiskey straight,
the blackout cocktails of oblivion.
He had *boozitis nervosa,*
an inflamed need for one down the hatch,
another for the road, a little pick me up
and on and on. Bad nerves.

Ray, the seller of shantung, pongee, peau de soie.
"The best for the best," he told his customers,
opening the sample book.
The bosses agreed Ray was number one, born for the job.
Yes, he liked a drink, no sourfaced teetotaler,
not Ray.

But when he mixed bicarb and raw eggs,
lemon and cayenne to swig in one gulp at seven A.M.,
Ray did the tremble step, the morning-after shuffle.
In a pure silk robe, toting up the sales, he began
to forget stops to make, calls to return.
Ray, a blurred man, slurring his words, missing the beat,
headed for the drying-out tank jamboree,
the nightmare delirum hop.

FAMILY LIFE

In his cups, he tore a twenty dollar bill
to make his mother, Nana, wince
unzipped his mouth and shrieked out: "bitch, you've ruined
everything, my goddamned life."
She turned her back to his whiskey breath,
and climbed the stairs like a martyred saint,
hummed a tune from the Hit Parade

while Dollie Dee in a purple snood was doing a samba
to Cugat's boom downstairs in the Whoopee Room;
lined up trophies from chug-a-lug beer fests, sozzled nights,
her maraschino cherry lips smeared in prints
at the edge of her glass, cocktail napkins, cigarettes.

Who was I to them? A guttersnipe, they said, one of the Pope's
unwanted, Brussels-born, a dingy sprout sitting in its dampness.
Dimwit music caving in my ears, snarls and battered silence,
I grew up hunched and humbled, pretended to forgive them—

but in dreams, Dollie fizzles and her hubby chokes
a wad of money down his throat.
"I've Got a Feeling I'm Falling," his mama croons,
standing tall as a post I must leap past to scrap the lessons
I learned by rote in that skewed house.

HEARING NEW YEAR'S EVE

Station WEAF, the announcer's voice
crackles into the kitchen with news
of the crowd, the clock, fireworks
at twelve when I almost see the old year
totter off, straggly beard and staff
flailing the air to the tune
of Auld Lang Syne's whiny throb
from the Rainbow Room.
Acquaintance be forgot. What?
What's out like a light?
Fumblers, barflies, my folks, their vows
to dry out. Hoarse from shouting, the night
closes its doors. Hangover blahs. Bromides
fizzle in a glass. Huddled in that kitchen
with its empty fridge, I stare
at the back end of the radio, and tubes glow
like a miniature city of pure glass towers
sending messages of years out to the stars.

THE HAPPY CHILD

No one need write HEAVEN in fluffed
white lines above the perfect town
her parents gave her
when she wanted a school
and regular bells.

Recently, white alphabets have entered
her house through front and back doors.
They tell her what to keep
like the fragrances of things
gone on before: cut hay, cake,
rain on wool sleeves.

This happy child leaping through hours
that end in a mist
of kisses her grateful parents give,
whatever she dreams,

she will wake in a scented bed
to a day like any other welcoming
her breath, new words, the light steps she takes
to run after moths, filaments of webs, the circling
shadow of a hawk . . .

but she cannot die like the unhappy child
waiting for rescue,
its mouth at the bottom of the well.
She can never be that urchin hurting
in the cramped, cool dark,
spewing up furious words
everyone ignores.

Off Central Park West, New York City

WHAT ARE THE DAYS

They are pilferers
stealing our resolve,
Thomas broods aloud.

Or stones
to use for good or ill,
says James sitting
on a rock with Peter.

Soon, the dreamer
comes along saying:
all days are brothers.

Aren't days fish
swimming to shore?
asks Simon, the fisherman
mending his nets.

They are coins to hoard
or to spend, Judas frowns,
and looks at his palms.

Twaddle, says Martha
running to fix supper.
You talkers, get me a hen,
get me an egg.

I bet you think
all the days are women
pouring wine and honey.

They are what they are,
says the hammerer of nails,
securing thieves
and the dreamer to the cross,
nothing more.

GOING FAR

My mother-in-law's dog ate stones.
After he died, my father-in-law left
twelve soap dishes and a sliver of soap.

When my husband was a boy,
alone and sinking in a lake,
a counselor happened by
and towed him to shore.

I almost drowned four times
from going out too far.
I didn't want to die.
I wanted to be recognized,
seaweed in my hair,
purple lips, sand in my nostrils,
for what I was: a bad swimmer,
a failed goddess.

In class, Mrs. Cole washed Richard Ryan's
mouth with soap for saying goddamn.

Once I swallowed stones on a dare.
It was heavy going to ride the waves
but I went far
and I am here, rescued from the past.
Goddamn!

READING TU FU, I WAIT FOR MY HUSBAND

Sequences, Autumn, Meditations, Tu Fu.
I read "a hundred years of the saddest news"
and "the forlorn boat, once and for all
tethers my homeward thoughts."

In the halflight of the booth,
thoughts sputter and leap. My fears are cast
to drift on a raft of words.
When will he arrive? Why is he late?
Reasons gather and disband.

Chang-an has dropped off the cliff
of a thousand years into powdery stones.
Stumps of memory grow in a weed-ridden garden.
The beautiful girls do not gather
kingfisher plumes as gifts
in the China of Deng Xiaoping.

Who will write we lived in a glorious age?
Where are the banners of Emperor Wu?
Tatters in the earth and under the stars
of The Seated Ministers
or placed on graves at the Festival of Tombs.

"Chanting, peering into the distance,
in anguish my white hair droops."
So Tu Fu ends his meditations,
the ones he wrote at K'uei-Chou in Seven Sixty-Six,
his second autumn in the region.

After I put the sequences away,
my attention narrows on a mirror image of myself
grown old, white-haired, waiting for my husband.
Suddenly, out of a shadowy corner, he appears
with a story of confusion and delay.
We kiss. It is our twentieth autumn in the city.

PROBINGS UNDER VEGA

When we lug the telescope up to the roof,
stars trapped in our lens, rightside left,
seem less real than their photographs
yet give joy like rare warblers sighted through binoculars.
Stars, birds, and their followers fly off
at different speeds. We will climb down a flight
of stairs, one foot at a time, heavy with gear.

Scroll or herald of fire, the sky transformed to metaphor
makes us ask what is real? Not the sense of our lives
deepened by shadows and given in an album of shots.
Not the album lying shut on its side
like a dreamer of bodies grouped here and there
at the beach, in a field flooded with light
from our middle-sized star.

Less vivid than our photographs, we stand in the dark
and are gazed upon and fastened to the shell of a far off,
blinding source. God as an infinite machine seems possible
as we look straight up at blue-white Vega, one-fourth the age
of the sun, twenty-six light years away,
brightest summer star.

SKYMYTHS

The six wives who ate onions are there
and the husbands who shoved them out of the hut,
long-haired Chasa arranges dew on stones and grass
for Chacaputi and his son, Topa.
The Tupi stargod, Maire-Monan, and one so large
the Zuni say his body can't be seen whole,
for his head sits in the west
while his heart beats at midheaven,
they are all there
reflected in the waters of the world,
in my bowl of facts, above our bluegreen ball
which will pass from vapor to ash
played by invisible lords of fate. They are there
in the trail of cornmeal drippings from the mouth of the dog,
in what Cherokee say of the Milky Way, the galaxy
the Yokut believe is dust from the race between antelope
and deer, a track made by snowshoes of a raven, the Inuit sing,
and the Fox's river of stars that sails above me, I, a person
of my tribe traveling from fire to fire, a wife,
onions on my tongue and a long mouth for speech.

RED AUGUST LETTER

Dear Friend:
The day you brought me geraniums,
my period came. That night I had a red dream,
red walls, lamps. You were a photographer
in a darkroom developing shots I couldn't
quite make out. I asked how you balanced
opposing needs. You shrugged and lifted
pictures out of a chemical bath.

In the photo you left of the party, who is
the feral-looking poet in the rumpled suit?
Woman hater? Once I would have memorized his poems.
The rain goes on. I've read your note, its chaste,
familiar script on a monogrammed blue page. I write.
My paper laps up ink. Stamps curl. A vague
taste of stickum lingers in my mouth.

Slack hours. Do you ever imagine the atoms
of your watch pulsing in a fading light?
Take a stand, intones my clock from its orderly
frontier. I resolve to reconcile odds and ends,
to inspect, put things out of sight, receive
the house-god, give him loose-skinned oranges,
an offering for auspicious news.

Was it last spring, after we'd found the cardinal's
nest fastened to a branch of pine, we spoke of ways
to stave off birth? What I didn't say was that
my scrap of a child sometimes floats in the back
of my head like a sea-creature, open-mouthed
as if it were startled or in pain to learn its
name would not be called.

Tonight Mars and Venus are aligned in the summer
sky. Come with your prints and films. All week
opulent sunsets have fallen on soaked roads.
Forecasters say nothing we haven't heard.
I want to hear your reflector dream, your daughter
dream, to be brought into communion with old ghosts.

AFTER THE CANTATA SOUNDS ITS LAST ALLELUIA

You slip off the headphones on your Walkman,
tell me it's Teresa Stich Randall singing
Bach's fifty-first. The room stirs
with the swirl of your pale hair,
the rustle of poems we hold up to light.

Facets, tone, breath, where the line breaks,
we hesitate, we leap. "Knife instead of poignard?"
"I hear *pond yard*," you explain.
I muse on the timbre of your voice,
coloratura soprano.

"Too many syllables . . . is it ornate?"
We volley phrases, suspended in the bubble
of an afternoon. Time neither flows nor ticks.
We look for the perfect pitch, the right note
to strike.

I mail you notes, one for every season.
You answer in your own time for a score
of reasons thrumming beyond these windows
that look out on five city trees
and a blue brick wall.

Spring. The sky's masonry seems built to last.
Today a note comes from my mother. The picture
she encloses of her father, Professor D., shows me
an elderly man with dreamy, half-closed eyes.

Carolyn, I imagine I see your father caught off-guard
in a snapshot. The sky shuffles little envelopes
of clouds over a tree-lined street. He squints
but can't read the letters of his daughter's name,
your old address shredding in the wind.

In my only picture of my father, his face is sad.
Sometimes, I brush my mouth over his lips
but he won't ever come to feel
the thin skin of my kiss.

Carolyn, when I caress the papery skin of your poems,
"ardent reds," vault into light,
a Joseph's coat of colors released
in waves like seeds or bees in summer fields.

"For the first time in my memory, the river
has frozen," my mother writes from another country.
Scenes of her past freeze in photographs
I frame in a revery:

With child, a young woman in a tight blue coat
boards a train for the city. On a tree-lined street
she turns to her lover who draws near and withdraws.
Their lovechild is offered to nuns who teach it
to sing for visitors: *Ave Maria* and *Minuit Chrétien.*
An old woman, she sits by the river in autumn
to write to a daughter she barely knows.

Carolyn, in a fiction I revise, our mothers and fathers
set down their papers and look at the light, day's end
sends them music in a white cloud of notes,
a cantata they have committed to heart to sing to us
out of all their lost seasons.

THE DAY WE MADE LONG SHADOWS

I thought I knew what I needed
to come through the winter. You.
Not suffering. I'd learned that
early on in shadowy aisles
of the church, in childhood's
noisy corridors.

Looking at our shadows,
"they pull darkness out of light,"
you said as we scuffed up sand
in a late afternoon of palms and gulls.

I knew our bodies defined them,
that they were ourselves obscure and pursued
in a tyranny of givens. I also wanted
what you knew.

"Explain them," I asked, and you drew
a circle of sun with angles to it
in the sand. Later, we spotted the shadow
of a pelican dipping its beak
at the sea's farthest edge.

WINTER MODES

What rose from those fallen days?
Tricks of light the ancients construed
as proof of doom or bliss.
We slept beneath the whale of night
and dreamed seven blue eggs in
The Pleiades would hatch blue fire
or damsel fish in a coral reef.

You said the saline level of primordial waters
was a quotient in our blood.
I tasted salt on your tongue.

Summer tides. The silver play of waves
whispered syllables of fish, sighs of lost
turtle years in underwater groves.
And inky clouds, the squids' defense
against insomniacal sharks.

In the jack pine, sparrows and jays
said who they were by their call.
Speedwell, lobelia grew in meadows we trailed.
We danced from happiness on the path to the sea
in that first summer of gazing at the Perseids,
of feeding anemones on the island rock pool.

Years later in winter, I ask if the nature
of snowflakes is known. You say temperature,
moisture, wind defines what transforms,
the single-planed, six-sided forms, not one
resembling the other since snow began.
You've gathered facts in a bouquet.

I ask you to look through the keyhole
to threadbare winters of another love.
Ragged snow, bridal lace. My fingers are almost blue
with cold on the January night I curse St. Agnes
for blessing my first union. When did I drop
the gold band in the sea?

Was it in summer? The residue of blasted stars
dims in my recollection of hungers and desires
before we married in July on the feast of St. Anne.
And in a union of circles moving towards their core,
I hold you fast, my love,
under the thorns of a red heaven
blooming planets and stars.

MUSING ON LARGE QUESTIONS IN
A SMALL CORNER OF ENGLAND

Early evening, firethorns, trillium.
In hedges goldfinch twitter.
And Blake in Felpham, dining naked
as Adam, I wonder when did he see
Druids gather in his garden?

The world's queries spin in books,
in motes above podiums, gold
in a hazy light.
Shelley breaking sponge cake
into hot rum and tea, why did he refute
logical proof in the notion of God?

Forgiving the plow, Blake's cutworms
do their work. And archangels sing
in the field. Is there no magic spell
to master death when it breaks loose?
The past curls away

but supping on violets, the Great Spangled
Fritillary can't deny anyone's reason for song
and lights one flower at a time in the meadow
like a flame.